Collins
revision guides

PracticePapers
KS3 English

Mike Gould

Published by HarperCollins*Publishers* Ltd
77-85 Fulham Palace Road
London W6 8JB

www.collinseducation.com
On-line support for schools and colleges

First published 2004

10 9 8 7 6 5 4 3 2 1

ISBN 0 00 717804 2

Mike Gould asserts the moral right to be identified as the author of this work.

British Library Cataloguing in Publication Data
A catalogue record for this book is available from the British Library.

Production by Katie Butler
Design by Chi Leung
Printed and bound by Printing Express, Hong Kong

Acknowledgements
The Author and Publishers are grateful to the following for permission to reproduce
copyright material:
Mary Evans Picture Library: p.14
Hodder & Stoughton: pp.10–11

Contents

What are the National Tests?

The education of children in the UK is divided into sections that are known as key stages. At infant and primary schools, children are at Key Stages 1 and 2. Secondary education begins with Key Stage 3 (KS3) and this covers the first three years of secondary schooling. We call these Years 7, 8 and 9. In Year 10 students move on to the next key stage, Key Stage 4. This is when students spend two years preparing for their GCSE examinations, which are completed in Year 11.

There are National Tests for all students that are organised by a government body known as the Qualifications and Curriculum Authority (QCA). These tests are designed to measure the progress students have made as they reach the end of a key stage. In the case of secondary schools, these KS3 tests (popularly know as SATs) are taken in May of Year 9. The test papers are marked externally, rather like GCSE examinations. The results are reported to schools and students before the end of the summer term, usually in early July.

Although schools are required to report their students' progress in all subjects, only three subjects are assessed by formal national tests. These subjects are:
- English;
- Mathematics;
- Science.

The National Tests in these subjects are not the only way in which the progress of each student is assessed.

Teacher Assessment

Teacher assessment is regarded as an essential part of the National Curriculum assessment and reporting arrangements, according to the QCA. Teachers must keep records of every student and update them regularly. All subjects, not just English, Mathematics and Science, include teacher assessment.

Attainment Targets

School subjects are divided into separate sections of work known as Attainment Targets. In each Attainment Target, or section of study, students may be working at different levels, according to their abilities. The levels each have a reference number. For example, a child may achieve level 4 in English at the end of primary schooling (the end of KS2). By the end of the key stage tests in Year 9, this child may have progressed to level 5, 6 or 7 within the same area of study.

The overall subject level achieved by a student will be calculated from the separate levels for each of the Attainment Targets. For example, in English, a child achieving levels 4, 5 and 6 in the three Attainment Targets, will be awarded the average, level 5.

English National Tests at KS3 (the Year 9 SATs)

The National Curriculum in English is divided into three Attainment Targets:

> En 1 Speaking and Listening
> En 2 Reading
> En 3 Writing

The Tests cover Reading and Writing. They also cover the Shakespeare play you have studied in Year 9, concentrating on the two scenes you have studied in detail. Your Listening and Speaking skills are not covered by the Tests, but are assessed by your teacher based on the work you have completed during the year.

In English, all students take the same Test papers, giving a National Curriculum level between 3 and 7.

There are **THREE** papers:

- The **Reading Paper**
- The **Writing Paper**
- The **Shakespeare Paper**

The Reading Paper

- There are three different texts or extracts for you to answer questions on. Two of these are **non-fiction**, and one is **fiction**.
- There are questions on different aspects of each text – about **20 questions in total**.
- It is worth **32 marks**.
- You have **1 hour 15 minutes** to read the extracts and answer the questions.

The Writing Paper

- There is **one** writing task, which asks you to write imaginatively about a set topic. You are free to choose the form of writing, as long as it is appropriate to the task.
- It is worth **30 marks**.
- You have **45 minutes** to complete the task (this includes **15 minutes** planning time).

The Shakespeare Paper

There are two sections to this paper: a short writing task, and a reading and understanding task about the Shakespeare play you have studied. You have **1 hour 15 minutes** to complete the tasks, including reading time.

The short writing task:

- There is **one** writing task (a report, letter, story, etc.). The **form** of the writing is specified and you **must** use that form.
- It is worth **20 marks**.
- It is on a **general theme** connected to the play you have studied (but you DO NOT have to refer to the play in order to answer the question!).

The reading and understanding task:

- There is **one** task which tests your **knowledge and understanding** of the Shakespeare play you have studied.
- It is worth **18 marks**.
- It is based on **two scenes** which you have studied in detail.

Total marks for the Test

Reading:	Reading paper	32
	Shakespeare: understanding	18
Writing	Longer writing task	30
	Shorter writing task	20
	TOTAL marks	**100**

How can I prepare for the English National Test?

This has book has been designed to help you prepare fully for your Key Stage 3 English Test. It does this by:

- giving you a chance to work through a practice paper, doing tasks that have been modelled on the real paper itself.

- pointing out key areas, skills and techniques that will assist you in fulfilling your potential.

- clarifying key elements of the Test so that you understand exactly what you are being asked to do.

- getting you to assess and evaluate your own performance so that you can work on weaknesses and build on strengths.

Therefore, the book provides:

- **A FULL practice paper**, in the identical format of the actual Test.

- **Individual mark schemes** for each part of the Test.

- **Guidance** and tips on how to tackle the test and get the best marks.

- **Model answers** which have been annotated for you to see what makes that answer achieve a certain level.

How should I use this book?

Question: **So, I've bought the book. Do I jump straight in and do the papers?**

Answer: Of course you can do this, but you wouldn't prepare for the real test in this way, would you? We suggest you do the following before you attempt the test:

- Read a range of short texts of different sorts and styles (magazine articles, letters to newspapers, junk mail, the openings of novels or short stories, perhaps even diary extracts from famous writers from the past).

- Look through your own English work, and try to identify where you have done well, and where you struggle. If you have done well on your Shakespeare work, then focus on reading modern non-fiction texts, perhaps –especially if that is an area where you have struggled.

Question: **Now I feel fairly well prepared. What now?**

Answer: Find yourself somewhere you can do the test in relative peace. The middle of the kitchen with the radio or TV blaring in the background might not be the best preparation!

Then, turn to the *Reading paper* and begin.

Question: **Why should I do the Reading paper first?**

Answer: You don't.You can choose to do whichever of the papers you want first. However, we would strongly advise you to do the Reading paper first for the simple reason that this will be the first paper you do when you do the 'real thing'.

Question: **Should I do all three papers in one go?**

Answer: Again, if you want to, but in the real test you will have a break between each paper. For example, you might do the *Reading paper* in the morning; the *Writing paper* in the afternoon; and the *Shakespeare paper* the next day. So, we suggest you do the same here. Do one paper, then have a break, then do the next – and so on.

However, it's worth doing all of one paper without stopping. Try not to stop after two questions for a cup of coffee! You won't be able to take a break in the middle of a real exam, so why do so now?

Question: **Right – that seems clear: do one paper at a time, taking a break in between. What about marking? The marking seems longer than the exam paper!**

Answer: The marking is long, and quite complicated, but – believe it or not – the mark schemes here are simplified ones so that you can get a basic indication of how you have done.

Question: I can't mark my own work, can I?

Answer: Why not? If you mark your own work, you are more likely to have to think about what you did right and wrong. However, if you feel uncomfortable doing so, ask a parent or even your teacher, if they wouldn't mind checking the work for you. But bear in mind that marking is not easy, and it will take time to do it.

Question: Is there anything else I should know?

Answer: Just make sure you read all the instructions for the test carefully, and take note of the advice that is given. If you do this, then you stand a good chance of doing well in the real test.

Good luck!

Reading paper

Are you being served?

There are **three extracts** for you to read and **answer questions** on (see below). The extracts are **all connected** by the **theme of being served by people** in shops or other places.

You have **1 hour and 15 minutes** to read the **three extracts** and answer **ALL** the questions.

Spend about **five minutes** reading **each text** before you write anything down.

Write **all your answers** down in **this book**.

When you have finished **CHECK** all your work carefully.

There are **14 questions** totalling **32 marks** on this paper.

The three extracts are:

Many people have experienced the good and bad side of being served in shops, restaurants or other places. Often, assistants are helpful and willing to sort out any problems, but on other occasions things can go wrong and customers and assistants both feel they have been badly treated.

So, what should customers do when they have problems with the objects they have bought, or with the people who serve them?

Buying: your rights

This extract comes from the Young Citizen's Passport: Your Guide to the Law *and explains what rights you have when you have a problem with something you have bought, and in particular the ways in which shops and businesses try to wriggle out of their obligations.*

Put downs

Some shops and firms will do as much as they can to help you with a problem over something you have bought, others may claim that there is nothing they can do. Don't give up if the shop tries to get out of its legal obligations.

We'll send it back to the workshop

Only if you want them to. If the fault appears shortly after you buy the goods and you haven't misused them, you need not face further inconvenience by having them repaired. You are entitled to your money back. But if the item worked well at first and then developed a fault, you may still be entitled to some or all of your money back, to be offered a replacement or to have it repaired free of charge. It all depends on how long you have had the goods, the seriousness of the fault and whether you

can convince the shop that it's not reasonable for a fault to develop so soon.

You'll have to take it up with the manufacturer

Wrong. You bought the goods from the shop. Your contract was with them, not a factory owner on the other side of the world. If the goods genuinely don't work, the shop has not kept its side of the contract and you have a right to your money back. The shop will have its own claim against its supplier.

We'll give you a credit note

No. If the goods are faulty, you're entitled to your money back. You don't have to accept a credit note.

Sorry, it's out of guarantee

This can be tricky. A major problem with an expensive computer three months after the guarantee has run out means a large repair bill. Raise it with the dealer and ask to talk to the manager. Produce the documentation and use the manufacturer's literature, (which probably stresses reliability and quality) to point out that it is not reasonable to expect a failure after such a short period. There's no hard and fast law

Sorry, it's out of guarantee

VCR

Guarantee Ran out yesterday!

We'll give you a replacement

We don't give refunds on sale goods

We'll give you a replacement

Only if that's what you want. However, if by now the fault has led you to decide that you don't really want the product after all, you are entitled to your money back – not a replacement. It's up to you to choose what to do.

about what is reasonable in terms of product failure. It depends on the circumstances.

We don't give refunds on sale goods

Wrong. Unless the fault was pointed out to you, or was something you should have seen when you bought them, goods bought in sales carry all the protection of the Sale of Goods Act 1979.

Finding it's wrong

If you are not satisfied with something that you have bought…

❶ Stop using it straightaway and take it back, with the receipt and the guarantee (if you have one), to the shop where you bought it. It strengthens your case if you can do this as soon as possible. Your contract was with the shop, not the manufacturer, so it is the shop's responsibility to deal with the complaint.

❷ Before you take the goods back, decide what you are going to say and what you would like the shop to do. Do you want your money back, or will you be happy to exchange the item for one that works?

❸ Think about your legal position. A faulty stop button on a personal stereo means that it is not of satisfactory quality. Don't be afraid to use the law when making your case.

❹ Keep calm. If the shop assistant doesn't help, ask for someone more senior.

❺ If you bought the goods by mail order or from a shop some distance away, it's easier to telephone or write. Keep a copy of all letters, send a photocopy of your receipt (keep the original), and if you talk on the phone get the name of the person you spoke to. Make a brief note of the conversation.

1. According to the first section, 'We'll send it back to the workshop' what are you entitled to if the fault appears shortly after you have bought the goods and you haven't misused them?

   ● _____

   1 mark

2. (a) In the section, 'Finding it's wrong', what **two** things should you decide **before** you take any faulty goods back?

   ● _____

   ● _____

   (up to 2 marks)

   (b) What do you think is the **main purpose** of this text?

   ● _____

   ● _____

   1 mark

3. Here are five suggested sub-headings to go with the numbered sections in 'Finding it's wrong'.

   Match the suggested sub-headings to the numbered sections in the text.

   Section 3 has already been matched for you.

Goods sent by post or from shops a long way away	☐
Using the law to help	3
Planning what to say when you go back to the shop	☐
How to behave in the shop	☐
What to do when you first discover a fault	☐

   2 marks

4. The writer uses different ways to make the advice given effective.

   (a) Explain how the writer's use of language makes the advice **clear** to the reader.
        Support your answer with at least one quotation.

   ● _____

   _____   *1 mark*

   (b) Explain how the writer tries to make the advice **practical** by **involving the reader**. Support your answer with at least one quotation.

   ● _____

   _____   *1 mark*

5. The overall impression given by the text is that the customer has rights and is in control when faulty goods are taken back.

   However, the writer does point out that sometimes things **aren't as straightforward**.

   Explain **three ways** in which the writer gives the impression customers may have problems in getting what they want.
   Support your answers with quotations from the text.

   ● _____

   _____

   _____

   ● _____

   _____

   _____

   ● _____

   _____

   _____   *3 marks*

A shared meal

In this extract from Charles Dickens' David Copperfield, *David has been sent away to school in London by his cruel stepfather. On the way, he stops at an inn and orders some food and drink. However, he is served by a waiter who takes advantage of his youth and innocence. In the extract you are about to read, the waiter has just told David that a man called Topsawyer drank the same ale as David the night before and then dropped down dead! The waiter offers to drink it as he is 'used to it'.*

I replied that he would much oblige me by drinking it, if he thought he could do it safely, but by no means otherwise. When he did throw his head back, and take it off quick, I had a horrible fear, I confess, of seeing him meet the fate of the lamented Mr Topsawyer, and fall lifeless on the carpet. But it didn't hurt him. On the contrary, I thought he seemed the fresher for it.

"What have we got here?" he said, putting a fork into my dish. "Not chops?"
"Chops," I said.
"Lord bless my soul!" he exclaimed, "I didn't know they were chops. Why a chop's the very thing to take off the bad effects of that beer! Ain't it lucky?"

So he took a chop by the bone in one hand, and a potato in the other, and ate away with a very good appetite, to my extreme satisfaction. He afterwards took another chop, and another potato; and after that another chop and another potato. When we had done, he brought me a pudding, and, having set it before me, seemed to ruminate, and to become absent in his mind for some moments.

"How's the pie?" he said, rousing himself.
"It's a pudding," I made answer.
"Pudding!" he exclaimed. "Why, bless me, so it is! What!" looking at it nearer. "You don't mean to say it's a batter-pudding!"
"Yes, it is, indeed."
"Why, a batter-pudding," he said, taking up a tablespoon, "is my favourite pudding! Ain't that lucky? Come on, little 'un, and let's see who'll get most."

The waiter certainly got most. He entreated me more than once to come in and win, but what with his tablespoon to my teaspoon, his despatch to my despatch, and his appetite to my appetite, I was left far behind at the first mouthful, and had no chance with him. I never saw any one enjoy a pudding so much, I think; and he laughed when it was all gone, as if his enjoyment of it lasted still.

Glossary

ruminate	meditate, think long and hard
entreated	begged or pleaded

Finding him so very friendly and companionable, it was then that I asked for the pen and ink and paper, to write to Peggotty. He not only brought it immediately, but was good enough to look over me while I wrote the letter. When I had finished it, he asked me where I was going to school.

I said, "Near London," which was all I knew.

"Oh, my eye!" he said, looking very low-spirited, "I am sorry for that."

"Why?" I asked him.

"Oh, Lord!" he said, shaking his head, "that's the school where they broke the boy's ribs - two ribs - a little boy he was. I should say he was let me see - how old are you, about?"

I told him between eight and nine.

"That's just his age," he said. "He was eight years and six months old when they broke his first rib; eight years and eight months old when they broke his second, and did for him."

I could not disguise from myself, or from the waiter, that this was an uncomfortable coincidence, and inquired how it was done. His answer was not cheering to my spirits, for it consisted of two dismal words, "With whopping."

The blowing of the coach-horn in the yard was a seasonable diversion, which made me get up and hesitatingly inquire, in the mingled pride and diffidence of having a purse (which I took out of my pocket), if there was anything to pay.

"There's a sheet of letter-paper," he returned. "Did you ever buy a sheet of letter-paper?"

I could not remember that I ever had.

"It's dear," he said, "on account of the duty. Threepence. That's the way we are taxed in this country. There's nothing else, except the waiter. Never mind the ink. I lose by that."

"What should you - what should I - how much ought I to - what would it be right to pay the waiter, if you please?" I stammered, blushing.

"If I hadn't a family, and that family hadn't the cowpock," said the waiter, "I wouldn't take a sixpence. If I didn't support a aged pairint, and a lovely sister" - here the waiter was greatly agitated - "I wouldn't take a farthing. If I had a good place, and was treated well here, I should beg acceptance of a trifle, instead of taking it. But I live on broken wittles - and I sleep on the coals" - here the waiter burst into tears.

I was very much concerned for his misfortunes, and felt that any recognition short of ninepence would be mere brutality and hardness of heart. Therefore I gave him one of my three bright shillings, which he received with much humility and veneration, and spun up with his thumb, directly afterwards, to try the goodness of.

Glossary

seasonable	timely, convenient
diffidence	timidity, uncertainty
cowpock	an infectious illness
pairint	the waiter's way of saying 'parent'.
wittles	food (from 'victuals' – an old word for food)

6. Give one detail from the first paragraph (**not** the introduction in italics) that shows that David is worried what might happen to the waiter when he drinks the ale.

   ● _____

     _____

     1 mark

7. In the paragraph beginning '*The waiter certainly got most*', how does the writer emphasise the difference between how much he gets, and how much the waiter gets? Explain **one way**.

   ● _____

     _____

     1 mark

8. In the section starting *There's a sheet of letter paper...*, explain how the choice of language in the following quotation shows us how David is feeling.

   Write down **two** ways his feelings are shown.

   "What should you - what should I - how much ought I to - what would it be right to pay the waiter, if you please?" I stammered, blushing.

   ● _____

     _____

   ● _____

     _____

     2 marks

9. From that same section (beginning *There's a sheet of letter-paper...*) to the end of the extract, how does the waiter fool David into paying him ninepence?

Write down **three** ways.

Support your answer with quotations.

● _____

_____

● _____

_____

● _____

_____

3 marks

10. The events of the extract could be summarised using the following headings.

Place them in the order in which they occur. ('A sad home life' refers to the waiter describing his misfortunes towards the end of the extract, so that is the last event – number 5.)

A school to be scared of?   ☐

Battle over a pudding   ☐

A sad home life   5

Saved by the coach   ☐

The dangers of drink   ☐

2 marks

The customer is always wrong

In this extract, a magazine writer, Chris Harris, decides to find out how customers are treated in his local high street.

My first port of call was a well-known department store on the high street, and my task was a simple one. I headed for the perfume counter, which was free of customers. Behind it was a woman wearing bright blue lipstick, and chewing some gum loudly. In front of her was a magazine, or something, and a large cup of coffee. A digital clock on the wall behind her read 11.07 am.

'Err. Excuse me,' I ventured.

She ignored me (or didn't hear me) and continued to look at *Hello!* magazine, or that month's issue of *Customer Care Monthly*, or whatever it was she was reading.

I coughed. She raised an eyebrow, but not an eye.

'Would you mind telling me where the toilets are?'

Slowly she raised her hand and pointed at me. This seemed rather strange, until I realised she was pointing over my shoulder, and out of the shop door. Clearly, she intended me to go back into the high street and walk half a mile to the public loos which everyone knows are always locked when you need them most.

'Actually, I meant the ones in here,' I persisted.

'5th floor,' she shot back, without raising her eyes from the catalogue.

'Thanks,' I said, and turned to leave. But as I did so, I saw the notice listing all the floors. There were only four. And it read: Toilets: 4th floor. I turned back to Miss Charming.

'Are you sure? It's just that it says....'

Now she fixed me with a look that could freeze burning oil in a chip-pan.

'It's the 5th floor, if you count the basement, which I always do.'

There was clearly no answer to this, but as I'd established (I think) where the toilets were, I decided it was time to move on. Looking back, I reckoned that she had actually helped me, albeit in her own sulky and mathematically-challenged way, so I put down a generous 6 out of 10 on my notepad.

Next stop was a small hardware shop. Worryingly, there were what looked like torture devices hanging from hooks on the walls, but behind the counter was a kindly-looking gentleman in a brown overall and wearing spectacles. He looked like your favourite uncle. Ah, this was more like it!

'Hello, sir. And what a very fine day it is today, isn't it?'

'Is it?' I responded, wondering how I had got soaked walking fifty metres from the department store to here.

'Oh, yes sir, we all like a bit of rain, don't we?'

Uh-oh. Now I recognised the type. This was the sort of assistant who only spoke in questions.

'Actually, that's why I'm here. Err – my conservatory roof is leaking, and I wondered what you'd recommend?'

He sighed as if I had asked him to tell me how to bring about world peace, and said,

'Well, that depends on the conservatory. Is it single or double-glazed? Is it UPVC or wood? Perspex or glass? Is the apex of the roof higher than the converse alignment of the lateral parallel frame circumference....?'

Actually, I made the last question up. In fact, it was more complicated than that. I looked at him blankly, and then pretended to check my watch.

'Is that the time? Just remembered I need to pick my wife up. I'll drop in another time...'

Even as I was leaving he was still firing questions at me.

'That wouldn't be Wednesday, would it? It's just we have half-day closing then, but shall I give you a ring when we're open? I mean, it's good to talk, isn't it?'

I stepped outside the shop, mentally giving him 7 out of 10 for persistence if nothing else. By then, I had already realised that there were two distinct groups of people in the world: customers and shop assistants. The shop assistants all thought the customers were brainless, and the customers thought all assistants were lunatics. The two I had met had been mad in different ways. Miss Charming was obviously completely unsuited to her profession – no wonder her perfume counter had been empty. On the other hand Mr Helpful would kill you with kindness and questions: you'd go in asking for a nail, and come out with a kitchen sink, a lawnmower, and an electric screwdriver with three hundred attachments.

So, I decided there and then, that any shopping would be done somewhere where no one spoke to you, or looked at you as if you were an alien from another plant. No, from that moment on, all my shopping would be done online, using the Internet. I mean, that couldn't possibly go wrong, could it? After all, machines aren't human, are they?

11. Suggest **two reasons** why the woman doesn't respond when the writer says 'Excuse me,' to her. Include quotations to support your answers.

● _____

   _____

● _____

   _____

2 marks

12. (a) How does the final paragraph of the article link with what has gone before? Write down **two ways**. Support your answers with quotations.

● _____

   _____

● _____

   _____

2 marks

(b) Based on how the last paragraph ends, what do you think is likely to happen when the writer orders his shopping online?

● _____

   _____

1 mark

13. What impression of the woman on the perfume counter is given by the writer's use of language?

_____

_____

_____

_____

_____

_____

_____

_____

_____

_____

_____

_____

_____

5 marks

14. The writer presents the situation in the hardware shop in a light-hearted or humorous way. Write down **two** examples of the use of humour in this section.

Support your answers with quotations.

● _____

_____

● _____

_____

2 marks

Total Score

maximum 32 marks

Reading paper: Answers and mark scheme

Here you can check your answers to the Reading paper, but remember – not every single answer possible has been given so, if you believe you have got the right answer, then give yourself the mark. Don't be too hard on yourself!

Buying: your rights

QUESTION 1
One mark for:

- You are entitled to your money back.

1 mark

QUESTION 2
2a)   **One mark** for **each** of these answers:
- What you are going to say

- What you would like the shop to do

2 marks

2b)   **One mark** for **any one** (or a **combination**) of the following:

- To give examples of the things shop assistants or workers might say, and explain what your rights are

- To show that not all shops or firms are helpful when you have problems with things you have bought

- To give practical advice on how to deal with shops or firms who deal in an unsatisfactory way with a problem you have with an item you have bought.

1 mark

QUESTION 3

One mark if **one** or **two sections** are correctly matched.
Two marks if **four sections** are correctly matched.

Goods sent by post or from shops a long way away	5
Using the law to help	3
Planning what to say when you go back to the shop	2
How to behave in the shop	4
What to do when you first discover a fault	1

2 marks

QUESTION 4

4a) **One mark** for either of these, or a combination of both:

- The writer uses simple, strong instructions such as *Keep calm/ Raise it with the dealer/Produce the documentation.*

- The writer uses clear organisational words and phrases to explain what to do *(if/But/However/So, etc).*

1 mark

4b) **One mark** for either of these, or a combination of both:

- The writer speaks to the reader directly *(You bought the goods/It's up to you.)*

- The writer provides examples of what the shop assistants might actually say when the reader speaks to them (**We'll** *give* **you** *a replacement).*

1 mark

QUESTION 5

One mark each for any **three** of the following:

- Faults aren't always reported immediately *(it all depends on how long you have had the goods.)*

- The faults aren't serious enough to complain about *(it all depends on....the seriousness of the fault)*

- Customers have to be quite strong-willed and convincing when they complain *(it all depends on...whether you can convince the shop...)*

- Customers' guarantees may have run out so they have to persuade the manager that it was unreasonable for the thing to break down *(This can be tricky/there's no hard and fast law/it all depends on circumstances)*

- Customers may have bought sale goods knowing the problems *(Unless the fault was pointed out to you...)*

- The writer uses words and phrases such as 'may', 'depends', 'whether', 'unless', which can suggest uncertainty.

> 3 marks

Key tip: **Check the marks carefully before you answer a question.** For example, although there are many possible answers to Question 5, only three are required. You will notice on the exam paper that space has been left for **three answers only**. Don't add others, and don't spend too long on this. If there are 32 marks for an exam of about an hour, then that's about TWO minutes per mark. So a question worth 2 marks should take you about four minutes to write.

A shared meal

QUESTION 6

One mark for **either** of the following answers:

- *He mentions that he's happy for him to drink it if he can do it safely.*

- *He says he has a 'horrible fear' that the waiter will meet the same fate as Mr Topswayer.*

> 1 mark

Question 7
One mark for **any one** of the following:

- He contrasts the waiter's tablespoon to his teaspoon
- He contrasts their appetites
- He contrasts their 'despatch' (quickness of eating)
- How David was 'left behind'
- How David had 'no chance'

1 mark

Question 8
One mark each for any **two** of the following:

- His inability to find the right words: *what should you – what should I – what would it be right to…etc* shows his uncertainty, and lack of experience in paying people
- His reference to 'the waiter' rather than 'you' shows that he finds the subject embarrassing.
- The fact that he 'stammered' and 'blushed' also shows his lack of experience and embarrassment.

2 marks

Question 9
One mark each for any **three** of the following:

- He tells him stamps are 'dear' (expensive) because of the tax.
- He makes him think he's paying little, by saying that he (the waiter) will pay for the ink! *Never mind the ink. I lose by that.*
- He makes David feel sorry for him by saying he has a family to support, including an 'aged pairint' and a 'lovely sister'.
- He also says they are ill – they have ' the cowpock'.
- He says he is treated badly by his employers (*If I had a good place, and was treated well here*)
- He says he only eats leftovers (*broken wittles*) and has an uncomfortable bed (*sleeps on the coals*)
- He bursts into tears.

3 marks

QUESTION 10

One mark if **one** or **two sections** are correctly matched.
Two marks if **four sections** are correctly matched.

A school to be scared of?	3
Battle over a pudding	2
A sad home life	5
Saved by the coach	4
The dangers of drink	1

2 marks

Key tip: A key assessment focus of all reading tests is to *deduce, infer and interpret information, events or ideas from texts*. In plain language, this means **make sense of things that aren't always obvious on first reading**. In 'A shared meal', there is nothing *directly* in the extract that says the waiter tricked David, but by looking at his behaviour, what he says, and how David responds, we can understand what the writer is trying to suggest to the reader. When we need to *interpret* a text the question we must ask ourselves is *why* did that character behave in that way?

The customer is always wrong

QUESTION 11

One mark each for any **two** of the following:

- She doesn't hear him because she is 'loudly chewing gum'.

- She ignores him because she's more interested in her magazine (*continued to look at Hello magazine...*).

- She ignores him because she is taking her mid-morning break (*the digital clock/the large cup of coffee*) in the shop!

2 marks

QUESTION 12

12a) **One mark** each for any **two** of the following:

- It begins with a reference to his last visit (*I stepped outside the shop, mentally giving him 7 out of 10 for persistence if nothing else.*).

- The writer comes to a conclusion based on his experiences (*By then, I had already realised...*).

- The writer sums up the two people he has met (*Miss Charming/ Mr Helpful*).

- His experiences make him decide to act differently in the future (*all my shopping would be done online...*)

> *2 marks*

12b) **One mark** for an answer such as:
- Although it doesn't say so, the rhetorical questions at the end (*I mean, that couldn't possibly go wrong, could it? After all, machines aren't human, are they?*) seems to be setting the writer up for a nasty shock or surprise.

> *1 mark*

QUESTION 13

The question asks: *What impression of the woman on the perfume counter is given by the writer's use of language?*

Here is some guidance on the sorts of things which you might put in your answer.

Up to **five marks** maximum.

1-2 marks: A basic answer which states that she is unhelpful, and not particularly welcoming to customers, and is also not especially bright. Few, if any quotations.

3-4 marks: Some understanding of how the writer uses language; mention of the woman's appearance and what she is doing (her *blue lipstick*, and her *chewing gum*, *reading*, etc.) which suggest she is bored, unhelpful, etc.

5 marks: For specific references to details such as *a look that could freeze burning oil in a chip-pan*, which suggests the woman really doesn't want to help. This might be supported by reference to the raised eyebrow (which usually signals disapproval) but '*not the eye*' (reluctance) and the reference as he leaves to *her own sulky and mathematically-challenged way* suggesting she is child-like, perhaps, and not very bright, though he doesn't actually say this. Also, his acceptance that she does actually help him, albeit not very usefully. Finally, the author's use of the ironic term *Miss Charming* suggesting she is the exact opposite.

> *5 marks*

QUESTION 14
One mark each for any **two** of the following:

- The reference to the '*torture devices*' contrasting with the kindly assistant.

- The man mentioning how it's '*a nice day*' despite the fact that the writer is soaked from the rain.

- The way the man only speaks in questions, and is still firing questions at him as he leaves.

- The description of how the man responds when he sighs '*…as if I had asked him to tell me how to bring about world peace*'.

- The way the writer makes up the answer the man gives (which is even more complicated!) '*Is the apex of the roof higher than the converse alignment of the lateral parallel frame circumference….?*'

> *2 marks*

Writing paper

There is **one task** which has **30 marks**. You have **45 minutes** to complete the paper, but this includes **15 minutes' planning time**.

So, spend about 5 minutes reading the question carefully, and about 10 minutes on writing your plan.

- **Plan your work** on the **planning page**.

- Write your answer on your own paper,

This is a test of **writing**, so remember that you will be marked on how well you:

- *structure your sentences and use punctuation – i.e. the variety of your sentences, and the way you organise words, phrases and sentences with punctuation.*

- *structure and organise the whole text – i.e. the overall way your text 'hangs together' (such as the way the paragraphs link with each other, where you place your ideas, etc.).*

- *use language and create the right tone/effect with your writing – i.e. making sure the text is suited to the purpose and 'sounds right'.*

When you have finished, **CHECK** all your work carefully.

Easy money?

You are the Assistant Manager of a large department store. Your boss, the manager, has sent you this note:

Dear Sam

I am worried about the way our staff employees are dealing with customers. I have had several complaints from members of the public about rudeness and lack of helpfulness.

Can you please spend the day observing staff in different parts of the store, and find out what is happening – are our staff really not up to the job?

Include any other comments from customers you speak to.

Please write me a report commenting on what you have found out.

Thanks

Glenda

Write the report for your manager, based on what you see during your day.

Use sub-headings to make your report clear.

30 marks

Use this page to plan your work (this page would not be marked in the test, but will help you structure your work).

- key details of how you spent your day to include in your first paragraph

- sub-headings to use throughout your report

- comments (good or bad) from customers

- key findings (what you found out)

Writing paper: mark scheme

Obviously, it is very difficult to give hard and fast advice about how well you did in this part of the test, but there *are* some key things that the better answers contain. What you need to look for is to what extent you have included these key things in *your* work.

Your work will be marked on **three** main areas:

A: Sentence structure and punctuation   *marks available: up to 8*

This means how **clearly organised**, **fluent** and **effective** your sentences are – for example:

- Have you used a **variety** of **sentence structures** (i.e. long, short, simple, complex) to fit the task?

- Have you used **suitable connectives** (joining words and phrases, such as *however, despite, in addition, etc*) to link sentences?

- Have you used **a variety of verbs** and **verb forms** to suit the writing task (for example, suitable tenses or 'mood' verbs (modals) such *as should, may, might, etc.*)?

- Have you used **punctuation** (full-stops, commas, semi-colons, etc.) to make meaning **clear**, or **for effect** (for example, exclamation marks for disbelief: *I was stunned!*)?

B: Text structure and organisation   *marks available: up to 8*

This means the **overall structure** and **shape** of the **whole text**, and how individual sections or ideas are **linked together** – for example:

- Have you written paragraphs with **clear links** to the **subject** you are writing about? (For example, if the report is about customer service, don't include a paragraph about the prices of goods, unless it is really relevant.)

- Are your main ideas **supported** by **evidence** or **other comments** or **details** (for example, *customers felt staff attitudes were unfriendly. As one woman said…*)?

- Have you made the reader **follow your line of thinking**? (For example, have you lead them towards the point you want to make?)

- Have you considered a **range** of **organisational devices**? (Remember: some texts use bullet points, sub-headings, numbering, etc.)

C: Composition and effect

Marks available: up to 14

This means the **appropriate style**, **form** and **language** for the text you are writing, matched to the **purpose** of the text, and where relevant, the **viewpoint** of the writer – for example:

- Does your **style match the form** of the text? (For example, if the form is an analytical business report, would a chatty, personal style be suitable?)

- Have you **maintained** this style **throughout** your piece?

- Have you **adapted** and **shaped** your writing to fit **the reader**? (For example, if you want to make an impact at the start have you put your most shocking/surprising finding at the beginning?)

- Have you used an **appropriate range** of **vocabulary** – **words**, **phrases** and **sentences** – to suit the form? (For example, in a report you might write, '*I have concluded from my analysis of the situation…*'.)

- Have you used **particular devices** to **interest** or **involve** the reader (where appropriate) – for example, by using rhetorical questions, or powerful images, or humour?

How do I know what level I have achieved from looking over my work?

Firstly, doing well – or badly – in one task does not mean you will automatically get a particular level. Your final mark is out of 100 (for Reading and Writing), so there are 50 marks available for Writing.

Of these 50 marks:

30 are available for the **main Writing task** (which you have just done) and **20** are available for the **shorter Writing task** in the **Shakespeare paper**.

So, you might get 20 for main task, but only 10 for the shorter task.

Your total of 30, however, would put you comfortably into the Level 6 band for Writing (based on the 2003 test results).

The table on the following page gives a broad indication of the marks available. It puts the three types of writing focus (Sentences, Text structure and Composition/effect) into one scheme.

Use this grid as a *broad* marking scheme for the main Writing Task you have just done. You may find some of the indicators a bit difficult to understand, but look at the text in brackets to see if this is like *your* work.

Level	Indicators	Marks
4	• Some links between what was seen and the effect (*David ignored her **so**….*) • Some variation in tense forms (*The effect on customers if this continues **will be**…*) • Most sentences correctly punctuated, and some use of other punctuation (i.e. inverted commas for direct speech). • Some use of paragraphs which have their own topics, some use of sub-headings etc, but limited control over how they are linked together • Some attempt to adopt role of Assistant Manager, but not much grasp of how he would write (*It was really awful the way the staff spoke*)	4-9
5	• Clear sense of chronology/order of events (***Firstly**, I observed the perfume counter…*) • Increasing confidence in use of connectives and links (*David failed to notice the customer, **consequently** she was annoyed **when…***) • Mix of topics for paragraphs –some reporting what was observed, some commenting on the situation. • Use of detail to support findings (***David explained that** the company should have provided him with…*) • Maintains report style throughout • An attempt to write as an Assistant Manager would actually write (suitably formal – *I recommend that…*) and a sense of his/her own response to the situation (*I was disappointed to see that..*) • Use of sub-headings, but with little thought	10-14
6	• Use of some modals, verb varieties to change meaning (*Things **would have been** much better in the toy department if…*) • Variety of paragraph, lengths and sections which can provide links of time (***Later**, in the sports department…*), cause/effect (***Because** of this…*) or contrast (***Although** the staff on the tills were friendly…*) • Some stylistic features to establish role of writer (i.e. as Assistant Manager – *Do we really want customers driven away by David's continual rudeness?*) • Some appropriate and concise descriptions (*the hard-working tills staff*) and appropriate specialist terms (*the staff quarters/Ground Floor/stock checking/in-store music* or similar) • Makes use of sub-headings, with some thought (i.e. different areas of store)	15-21

Level	Indicators	Marks
7	• Sentences used for emphasis and effect, with a variety of sentence starters (*On approaching the store entrance, I felt increasingly uneasy. Was the store really as bad as suggested?*) • Complex verb forms, used confidently (**Had it not been for the till**, *it would have been impossible to tell this was the Customer Service area.*) • Wide range of punctuation, often used for effect (i.e. semi-colon used to balance ideas in a sentence) • Direct and reported speech, where appropriate (*David told me that…David said, 'There's too much to do.'*) • The report is well organised, makes use of sub-headings as suggested (but also considers order or content of heading) and works towards a final conclusion or statement. • Appropriate style and description chosen carefully to appeal to the readership (the Manager). For example, *If we want this flagship store to thrive we will all have to pull together…* + use of range of devices (i.e. rhetorical) to make comments clear (*What did I find? A member of staff using her mobile phone!*)	22+

MODEL RESPONSE

To: Glenda
From: Sam

Re: Customer complaints in the store

As requested, I can now report on the state of customer relations as I observed it. This report is based on a morning spent firstly on the ground and first floors, and an afternoon spent on the third floor and the top floor restaurant.

First impressions
I decided to begin my analysis of the store from the outside and see what initial impression was gained. I have to admit that I feared the worst, and I am relieved to report that on entering the store, the first impressions gained were good: the staff in Accessories were all present, and either **gainfully employed** on some task or other (Helen was altering a scarf display) or **dealing pleasantly with customers**. **Notices were clear, as was pricing**.

The first floor
However, my experiences on the first floor were somewhat less promising. **What did I find?** A member of staff using her mobile phone to make a private call, while a small queue of customers formed. She was entirely unaware of their presence until one of them spoke to her tentatively. Even then she seemed to be irritated that they had interrupted more important business. **It would be wrong** to rush to judgement – the person in question may have been talking to a sick relative, or going through some sort of personal crisis, but we should discuss the matter with her. It is the only option.
Other staff seemed equally unhelpful. One customer said to me, '**You'd think they'd be pleased we want to buy things!**' She didn't realise I was a member of staff. I received similar comments from a range of customers on the first floor.

The afternoon
I remained on the first floor until the end of the morning, and moved around all departments. The only one where the service could be described as satisfactory, in my opinion, was Menswear, although this was rather difficult to ascertain due to a general lack of customers.

For lunch, I went up the restaurant. Fortunately, this was **a beacon of light** in more ways than one. It was clean, yet buzzing with activity. The staff serving were friendly and the food looked appetizing and worth the money. Families, couples – indeed, a whole range – were eating there. I spoke to one young mother who admitted she hadn't bought anything from the shop but often used the restaurant to feed her young ones, as it was such good value and so pleasant!

End of the day
I finished the day by descending to the second floor. This proved to be a mistake. The department I entered – Sportswear – had no one on the till; in fact had it not been for the till, there would have been no way of telling that this was the Customer Service area! I looked in vain for staff, and was still looking when the voice came over the in-store speakers saying the store was about to close.

In conclusion
I recognise that this is only a snapshot of what the store offers, and perhaps on another day I would have had a more positive experience. However, if we want this **flagship** store to thrive, we will all need to pull together. We must all take an example from the restaurant and ground floor staff, who, **on this evidence**, are what keeps this store running.

Introduction sets out purpose and sums up what was done.

Appropriate sub-heading.

Correct tone and style for report

Connective for new section signals change

Use of question to engage reader

Use of modal 'would' suggests caution

Examples given to support viewpoint

Direct quotation from customer, as requested in task

Useful and appropriate description

Semi-colon usefully divides sentence, linking statement with explanation

Appropriate and vivid noun to convey writer's feeling

Links conclusion to earlier findings

Shakespeare paper

The paper is **1 hour 15 minutes** long.

You may choose to write about **one** of **three** Shakespeare plays.

- *Macbeth*
- *Twelfth Night*
- *Henry V*

Whichever Shakespeare play you choose, the paper has **two sections**:

Section A assesses your writing and has **20 marks**;
Section B assesses your reading and understanding of your chosen play, and has **18 marks**.

Turn to **page 40** for the *Macbeth* paper.

Turn to **page 46** for the *Twelfth Night* paper.

Turn to **page 52** for the *Henry V* paper.

Tips for the Shakespeare paper

Remember!
The Shakespeare paper is testing you on TWO areas:

- Writing

- Reading.

Section A: Writing

- The first, 'short' task (Section A) is testing your **Writing skills**.

- You **DO NOT write about the Shakespeare play** you are studying.

- It is just being used as a way of **making you think** about an idea or issue.

You will be awarded marks for the following:

- Sentence structure, punctuation and text organisation: *up to 6 marks*

- Composition and effect   *up to 10 marks*

- Spelling   *up to 4 marks*

TIPS

1 First, **read** the Writing task/question **carefully** and **ask yourself**:

What sort of text am I expected to write?   Example: *letter? story?*

What is the *purpose* of the text?   Example: *explain? Persuade?*

Who is the *audience*?   Example: *local people? children?*

2 Think **quickly** about the **style/language** expected: Example: *formal? chatty?*

3 Write your text, and **as you write**:

- **refer back** to the task/question to make sure you are on track

- be aware of **who you are writing for**, and the **purpose**

- check **paragraphs**, **sentences** and **spelling** as you go along.

4 Don't spend more than 30 minutes on this task, or you won't have enough time left to write a good answer to the question on your Shakespeare play.

Section B: Reading

- Answer on **the play you have studied**.

- There is only **one question**.

- This is a **test of Reading**, but this doesn't mean you should write untidily!

You will be awarded **up to 18 marks** for the following:

- **Clear understanding of the language and events** of the play and the scenes you are writing about

- **Relevant and carefully-selected comments** supported by **examples** and/or direct **quotations** from the play

- (Usually) reference to **how characters or ideas are presented** to the reader/audience

- **Clear expression:** this is a test of reading but your writing must be easy to follow and your ideas need to be expressed fluently.

TIPS

1 As always, **read the task/question carefully. Note the key words** and work out exactly what you have to do.

For example, if the question asks you what **different** impressions we get of a character, make sure you write about the character in different ways, showing how he/she changes.

2 Organise your answer sensibly into **clear paragraphs** and **sentences**.

For example, **link** your **ideas** where you can, so that the reader is quite clear what you mean: *In Act 1 Scene 3 Macbeth seems startled and shocked by what the witches seem to be offering, **therefore** it is a surprise when later in the play he...*

3 Support what you say with **quotations** and **references** from the extracts.

For example, you can:
- **sum up** what has happened in your own words, adding any evidence for your thoughts;
- **paraphrase** what someone says in order to support an idea (*Clearly Macbeth is full of anxiety when he tells Lady Macbeth what he is feeling*).
- **quote directly** (*Macbeth is full of anxiety about what he has done, saying that his mind is 'full of scorpion'.*

Macbeth: Section A – Writing

You should spend about 30 minutes on this section.

The play *Macbeth* starts with Macbeth and his friend meeting three strange women on their way back from the battle.

Strange meeting

Imagine you are a professional writer. You have received the following letter from a book publisher.

I am putting together a collection of stories called 'Strange meetings'.

The stories must be about a traveller or travellers, who meet strange people during a journey. Can you please write the opening of one of these stories, and send it to me? If I like the opening, I will ask you to write the whole story to include in the book.

Yours sincerely

David Lyons
Book Publisher

Write the opening to your story. Remember: it must be about a traveller (or travellers) who meets someone strange or unusual on his/her journey.

20 marks including 4 for spelling

Section B – Reading

You should spend about 45 minutes on this section.

Macbeth

Act 1 Scene 3, lines 98 to 155
Act 3 Scene 1, lines 19 to 73

What differences are there in Macbeth's attitude to Banquo in these two extracts?

Support your ideas by referring to the extracts which are printed on the following pages.

---

18 marks

Macbeth

Act 1 Scene 3, lines 98 to 155

> In this extract Angus and Ross, two noblemen, have just met up with Macbeth and Banquo, and are about to give them some news.

ANGUS	We are sent
	To give thee from our royal master thanks;
	Only to herald thee into his sight, 100
	Not pay thee.

ROSS	And, for an earnest of a greater honour,
	He bade me, from him, call thee thane of Cawdor:
	In which addition, hail, most worthy thane!
	For it is thine.

BANQUO   What, can the devil speak true?   105

MACBETH   The thane of Cawdor lives: why do you dress me
In borrow'd robes?

ANGUS	Who was the thane lives yet;
	But under heavy judgment bears that life
	Which he deserves to lose.
	Whether he was combined with those of Norway, 110
	Or did line the rebel with hidden help
	And vantage, or that with both he labour'd
	In his country's wreck, I know not;
	But treasons capital, confess'd and proved,
	Have overthrown him.

MACBETH	[*Aside*] Glamis, and thane of Cawdor! 115
	The greatest is behind.
	[*To ROSS and ANGUS*] Thanks for your pains.
	[*To BANQUO*] Do you not hope your children shall be kings,
	When those that gave the thane of Cawdor to me
	Promised no less to them?

BANQUO	That trusted home
	Might yet enkindle you unto the crown, 120
	Besides the thane of Cawdor. But 'tis strange:
	And oftentimes, to win us to our harm,
	The instruments of darkness tell us truths,
	Win us with honest trifles, to betray's
	In deepest consequence.
	Cousins, a word, I pray you.

MACBETH [*Aside*]   Two truths are told,
As happy prologues to the swelling act
Of the imperial theme.–I thank you, gentlemen.
[*Aside*] This supernatural soliciting
Cannot be ill, cannot be good: if ill,   130
Why hath it given me earnest of success,
Commencing in a truth? I am thane of Cawdor:
If good, why do I yield to that suggestion
Whose horrid image doth unfix my hair
And make my seated heart knock at my ribs,   135
Against the use of nature? Present fears
Are less than horrible imaginings:
My thought, whose murder yet is but fantastical,
Shakes so my single state of man that function
Is smother'd in surmise, and nothing is   140
But what is not.

BANQUO Look, how our partner's rapt.

MACBETH [*Aside*] If chance will have me king, why, chance may crown me,
Without my stir.

BANQUO   New honours come upon him,
Like our strange garments, cleave not to their mould
But with the aid of use.

MACBETH [*Aside*] Come what come may,   145
Time and the hour runs through the roughest day.

BANQUO Worthy Macbeth, we stay upon your leisure.

MACBETH Give me your favour: my dull brain was wrought
With things forgotten. Kind gentlemen, your pains
Are register'd where every day I turn   150
The leaf to read them. Let us toward the king.
Think upon what hath chanced, and, at more time,
The interim having weigh'd it, let us speak
Our free hearts each to other.

BANQUO Very gladly.

MACBETH Till then, enough. Come, friends.   155

Exeunt

Macbeth

Act 3 Scene 1, lines 19 to 73

In this extract, Macbeth asks Banquo what his plans are for the day, and reminds him of the banquet that evening.

MACBETH	Ride you this afternoon?	
BANQUO	Ay, my good lord.	20
MACBETH	We should have else desired your good advice, Which still hath been both grave and prosperous, In this day's council; but we'll take to-morrow. Is't far you ride?	
BANQUO	As far, my lord, as will fill up the time 'Twixt this and supper: go not my horse the better, I must become a borrower of the night For a dark hour or twain.	25
MACBETH	Fail not our feast.	
BANQUO	My lord, I will not.	30
MACBETH	We hear, our bloody cousins are bestow'd In England and in Ireland, not confessing Their cruel parricide, filling their hearers With strange invention: but of that to-morrow, When therewithal we shall have cause of state Craving us jointly. Hie you to horse: adieu, Till you return at night. Goes Fleance with you?	35
BANQUO	Ay, my good lord: our time does call upon's.	
MACBETH	I wish your horses swift and sure of foot; And so I do commend you to their backs. Farewell.	40

Exit BANQUO

Let every man be master of his time
Till seven at night: to make society
The sweeter welcome, we will keep ourself
Till supper-time alone: while then, God be with you!   45

Exeunt all but MACBETH, and an attendant

Sirrah, a word with you: attend those men
Our pleasure?

ATTENDANT They are, my lord, without the palace gate.

MACBETH Bring them before us.

Exit Attendant

             To be thus is nothing;
But to be safely thus.—Our fears in Banquo   50
Stick deep; and in his royalty of nature
Reigns that which would be fear'd: 'tis much he dares;
And, to that dauntless temper of his mind,
He hath a wisdom that doth guide his valour
To act in safety. There is none but he   55
Whose being I do fear: and, under him,
My Genius is rebuked; as, it is said,
Mark Antony's was by Caesar. He chid the sisters
When first they put the name of king upon me,
And bade them speak to him: then prophet-like   60
They hail'd him father to a line of kings:
Upon my head they placed a fruitless crown,
And put a barren sceptre in my gripe,
Thence to be wrench'd with an unlineal hand,
No son of mine succeeding. If 't be so,   65
For Banquo's issue have I filed my mind;
For them the gracious Duncan have I murder'd;
Put rancours in the vessel of my peace
Only for them; and mine eternal jewel
Given to the common enemy of man,   70
To make them kings, the seed of Banquo kings!
Rather than so, come fate into the list.
And champion me to the utterance! Who's there!

Re-enter Attendant, with two Murderers

Section A – Writing

You should spend about 30 minutes on this section.

In *Twelfth Night*, Malvolio believes he has been wrongfully imprisoned because Maria and Sir Toby played a trick on him. There are many cases of wrongful imprisonment in the world today.

Wrongful imprisonment!

You are a reporter for a local newspaper. The editor of your newspaper sends you this email:

From: The Editor
Subject: Imprisonment error
Date: 12 August 9 am

A lady called Mrs Piper has just phoned to say her husband, Dennis Piper, 79, has been held in jail overnight by the police. He was accused of stealing a police car and driving it along a motorway on the wrong side! The police have just realised that they arrested the *wrong* Mr Piper. The Mr Piper they wanted was actually a youth aged 17! They are about to release the innocent Mr Piper.

Get down to the police station and find out what happened.

Write the report for the front page. Make sure you include (old) Mr Piper's views, and explain why he was arrested.

20 marks including 4 marks for spelling

Section B – Reading

You should spend about 45 minutes on this section.

Twelfth Night

Act 2 Scene 3, lines 83 to 143
Act 4 Scene 2, lines 20 to 69

From these two extracts, what different impressions do we get of Malvolio?

Support your ideas by referring to the extracts which are printed on the following pages.

18 marks

Twelfth Night

Act 2 Scene 3, lines 83 to 143

> In this extract, Sir Toby, Feste, Sir Andrew and Maria have been drinking and singing late at night. Malvolio enters and tells them what he thinks of their behaviour.

Enter MALVOLIO

MALVOLIO My masters, are you mad? or what are you? Have ye no wit, manners, nor honesty, but to gabble like tinkers at this time of night? Do ye make an alehouse of my lady's house, that ye squeak out your coziers' catches without any mitigation or remorse of voice? Is there no respect of place, persons, nor time in you?

SIR TOBY We did keep time, sir, in our catches. Sneck up!

MALVOLIO Sir Toby, I must be round with you. My lady bade me tell you, that, though she harbours you as her kinsman, she's nothing allied to your disorders. If you can separate yourself and your misdemeanours, you are welcome to the house; if not, an it would please you to take leave of her, she is very willing to bid you farewell.

SIR TOBY 'Farewell, dear heart, since I must needs be gone.'

MARIA Nay, good Sir Toby.

FESTE 'His eyes do show his days are almost done.'

MALVOLIO Is't even so?

SIR TOBY 'But I will never die.'

FESTE Sir Toby, there you lie.

MALVOLIO This is much credit to you.

SIR TOBY 'Shall I bid him go?'

FESTE 'What an if you do?'

SIR TOBY 'Shall I bid him go, and spare not?'

FESTE 'O no, no, no, no, you dare not.'

SIR TOBY Out o' tune, sir: ye lie. Art any more than a steward? Dost thou think, because thou art virtuous, there shall be no more cakes and ale?

FESTE   Yes, by Saint Anne, and ginger shall be hot i' the mouth too.

SIR TOBY   Thou'rt i' the right. Go, sir, rub your chain with crumbs. A stoup of wine, Maria!

MALVOLIO   Mistress Mary, if you prized my lady's favour at anything more than contempt, you would not give means for this uncivil rule: she shall know of it, by this hand.

Exit

MARIA   Go shake your ears.

SIR ANDREW   'Twere as good a deed as to drink when a man's a-hungry, to challenge him the field, and then to break promise with him and make a fool of him.

SIR TOBY   Do't, knight: I'll write thee a challenge: or I'll deliver thy indignation to him by word of mouth.

MARIA   Sweet Sir Toby, be patient for tonight: since the youth of the count's was today with thy lady, she is much out of quiet. For Monsieur Malvolio, let me alone with him: if I do not gull him into a nayword, and make him a common recreation, do not think I have wit enough to lie straight in my bed: I know I can do it.

SIR TOBY   Possess us, possess us; tell us something of him.

MARIA   Marry, sir, sometimes he is a kind of puritan.

SIR ANDREW   O, if I thought that, I'd beat him like a dog!

SIR TOBY   What, for being a puritan? thy exquisite reason, dear knight?

SIR ANDREW   I have no exquisite reason for't, but I have reason good enough.

MARIA   The devil a puritan that he is, or any thing constantly, but a time-pleaser; an affectioned ass, that cons state without book and utters it by great swarths: the best persuaded of himself, so crammed, as he thinks, with excellencies, that it is his grounds of faith that all that look on him love him; and on that vice in him will my revenge find notable cause to work.

Twelfth Night

Act 4 Scene 2, lines 20 to 69

> In this extract, Malvolio has been imprisoned for his 'mad' behaviour. Feste has dressed up as a curate (a religious man) called Sir Topaz, sent to test his sanity.

MALVOLIO   [*Within*] Who calls there?

FESTE   Sir Topas the curate, who comes to visit Malvolio the lunatic.

MALVOLIO   Sir Topas, Sir Topas, good Sir Topas, go to my lady.

FESTE   Out, hyperbolical fiend! how vexest thou this man! Talkest thou nothing but of ladies?

SIR TOBY   Well said, Master Parson.

MALVOLIO   Sir Topas, never was man thus wronged: good Sir Topas, do not think I am mad: they have laid me here in hideous darkness.

FESTE   Fie, thou dishonest Satan! I call thee by the most modest terms; for I am one of those gentle ones that will use the devil himself with courtesy: sayest thou that house is dark?

MALVOLIO   As hell, Sir Topas.

FESTE   Why it hath bay windows transparent as barricadoes, and the clerestories toward the south north are as lustrous as ebony; and yet complainest thou of obstruction?

MALVOLIO   I am not mad, Sir Topas: I say to you, this house is dark.

FESTE   Madman, thou errest: I say, there is no darkness but ignorance; in which thou art more puzzled than the Egyptians in their fog.

MALVOLIO   I say, this house is as dark as ignorance, though ignorance were as dark as hell; and I say, there was never man thus abused. I am no more mad than you are: make the trial of it in any constant question.

FESTE   What is the opinion of Pythagoras concerning wild fowl?

MALVOLIO   That the soul of our grandam might haply inhabit a bird.

FESTE   What thinkest thou of his opinion?

MALVOLIO   I think nobly of the soul, and no way approve his opinion.

FESTE   Fare thee well. Remain thou still in darkness: thou shalt hold
the opinion of Pythagoras ere I will allow of thy wits, and fear to kill a
woodcock, lest thou dispossess the soul of thy grandam. Fare thee well.

MALVOLIO   Sir Topas, Sir Topas!

SIR TOBY   My most exquisite Sir Topas!

FESTE   Nay, I am for all waters.

MARIA   Thou mightst have done this without thy beard and gown: he sees
thee not.

SIR TOBY   To him in thine own voice, and bring me word how thou findest him:
I would we were well rid of this knavery. If he may be conveniently
delivered, I would he were, for I am now so far in offence with my
niece that I cannot pursue with any safety this sport to the upshot.
Come by and by to my chamber.

Exeunt SIR TOBY and MARIA

Section A – Writing

You should spend about 30 minutes on this section.

The King, in *Henry V*, shows mercy (to the drunk who insults him) and no mercy whatsoever to the three traitors, the French prisoners or Bardolph.

No mercy?

Imagine you work at a Youth Club. One night, when you are at home, you receive an email from the manager.

To: Ali
Date: 14 June
Subject: Advice please

I have just caught one of our new members stealing money (about £50) from the office. This was money the club raised to pay for a new CD player. This person promises that they will never do it again if I let them off this time. However, perhaps I should call the police? What do you think I should do?

Email me back with some advice.

Thanks for your help.

Jo

Write the email to your manager giving your advice. <u>Do not</u> use abbreviated words or phrases (e.g. C.U for See you).

20 marks including 4 marks for spelling

Section B – Reading

You should spend about 45 minutes on this section.

Henry V

Act 3 Scene 1 (not Chorus), lines 1 to 34
Act 4 Scene 7, lines 45 to 104

What different impressions of war are given in these two extracts?

Support your ideas by referring to the extracts which are printed on the following pages.

---

18 marks

Henry V

Act 3 Scene 1, lines 1 to 34

In this extract, Henry speaks to his soldiers as they attack the town of Harfleur.

SCENE I. France. Before Harfleur.

Alarum. Enter KING HENRY, EXETER, BEDFORD, GLOUCESTER, and Soldiers, with scaling-ladders

KING	Once more unto the breach, dear friends, once more;	
	Or close the wall up with our English dead.	
	In peace there's nothing so becomes a man	
	As modest stillness and humility:	
	But when the blast of war blows in our ears,	*5*
	Then imitate the action of the tiger;	
	Stiffen the sinews, summon up the blood,	
	Disguise fair nature with hard-favour'd rage;	
	Then lend the eye a terrible aspect;	
	Let pry through the portage of the head	*10*
	Like the brass cannon; let the brow o'erwhelm it	
	As fearfully as doth a galled rock	
	O'erhang and jutty his confounded base,	
	Swill'd with the wild and wasteful ocean.	
	Now set the teeth and stretch the nostril wide,	*15*
	Hold hard the breath and bend up every spirit	
	To his full height. On, on, you noblest English.	
	Whose blood is fet from fathers of war-proof!	
	Fathers that, like so many Alexanders,	
	Have in these parts from morn till even fought	*20*
	And sheathed their swords for lack of argument:	
	Dishonour not your mothers; now attest	
	That those whom you call'd fathers did beget you.	
	Be copy now to men of grosser blood,	
	And teach them how to war. And you, good yeoman,	*25*
	Whose limbs were made in England, show us here	
	The mettle of your pasture; let us swear	
	That you are worth your breeding; which I doubt not;	
	For there is none of you so mean and base,	
	That hath not noble lustre in your eyes.	*30*
	I see you stand like greyhounds in the slips,	
	Straining upon the start. The game's afoot:	
	Follow your spirit, and upon this charge	
	Cry 'God for Harry, England, and Saint George!'	

Exeunt. Alarum, and chambers go off

Henry V

Act 4 Scene 7, lines 45 to 104

In this extract, which follows the Battle of Agincourt, Henry learns of the killing of the boys, and speaks about the battle with his soldiers.

Alarum. Enter KING HENRY, and forces; WARWICK, GLOUCESTER, EXETER, and others

KING	I was not angry since I came to France	45
	Until this instant. Take a trumpet, herald;	
	Ride thou unto the horsemen on yon hill:	
	If they will fight with us, bid them come down,	
	Or void the field; they do offend our sight:	
	If they'll do neither, we will come to them,	50
	And make them skirr away, as swift as stones	
	Enforced from the old Assyrian slings:	
	Besides, we'll cut the throats of those we have,	
	And not a man of them that we shall take	
	Shall taste our mercy. Go and tell them so.	55

Enter MONTJOY

EXETER Here comes the herald of the French, my liege.

GLOUCESTER His eyes are humbler than they used to be.

KING How now! what means this, herald? Know'st thou not
That I have fined these bones of mine for ransom?
Comest thou again for ransom?

MONTJOY	No, great king:	
	I come to thee for charitable licence,	60
	That we may wander o'er this bloody field	
	To look our dead, and then to bury them;	
	To sort our nobles from our common men.	
	For many of our princes–woe the while!–	65
	Lie drown'd and soak'd in mercenary blood;	
	So do our vulgar drench their peasant limbs	
	In blood of princes; and their wounded steeds	
	Fret fetlock deep in gore and with wild rage	
	Yerk out their armed heels at their dead masters,	70
	Killing them twice. O, give us leave, great king,	
	To view the field in safety and dispose	
	Of their dead bodies!	

KING   I tell thee truly, herald,
I know not if the day be ours or no;
For yet a many of your horsemen peer   75
And gallop o'er the field.

MONTJOY   The day is yours.

KING   Praised be God, and not our strength, for it!
What is this castle call'd that stands hard by?

MONTJOY   They call it Agincourt.

KING   Then call we this the field of Agincourt,   80
Fought on the day of Crispin Crispianus.

FLUELLEN   Your grandfather of famous memory, an't please your majesty,
and your great-uncle Edward the Plack Prince of Wales, as I have
read in the chronicles, fought a most prave pattle here in France.

KING   They did, Fluellen.   85

FLUELLEN   Your majesty says very true: if your majesties is remembered of
it, the Welshmen did good service in a garden where leeks did
grow, wearing leeks in their Monmouth caps; which, your
majesty know, to this hour is an honourable badge of the service;
and I do believe your majesty takes no scorn to wear the leek   90
upon Saint Tavy's day.

KING   I wear it for a memorable honour;
For I am Welsh, you know, good countryman.

FLUELLEN   All the water in Wye cannot wash your majesty's Welsh plood
out of your pody, I can tell you that: God pless it and preserve   95
it, as long as it pleases his grace, and his majesty too!

KING   Thanks, good my countryman.

FLUELLEN   By Jeshu, I am your majesty's countryman, I care not who
know it; I will confess it to all the 'orld: I need not to be
ashamed of your majesty, praised be God, so long as your   100
majesty is an honest man.

KING   God keep me so! Our heralds go with him:
Bring me just notice of the numbers dead
On both our parts.

Section A - Writing

Because this is an 'essay-style' task, it is difficult to provide hard and fast rules about what marks you will get. However, use the following as broad guidance when looking over the work you have done.

The whole task is **marked out of 20**. Remember, marks are awarded for:

Sentence structure, punctuation and text organisation *marks available: up to 6*
Composition and effect *marks available: up to 10*
Spelling *marks available: up to 4*

Use the grids below as a *broad* marking scheme for the short Writing Task you have just done.

SENTENCE STRUCTURE, PUNCTUATION AND TEXT ORGANISATION

Level	Indicators	Marks
4	• Sentences mostly correct in terms of grammar • There is some variation in the way you start them (e.g. *Despite this...*) • Punctuation of sentences mostly correct, using not just full-stops • Tenses used for the order things happen (e.g *When you have finished, go and...*)	1-2
5	• You change sentence structures deliberately to create impact on your reader • Almost all your sentences are correctly punctuated, using a range of punctuation • Some variation in types of verb you use, to change their effect (e.g. using *would, will*, etc)	3-4
6	• You use a variety in the length and structure of your sentences for effect • Your ideas are linked together or organised within paragraphs to aid the meaning you are trying to convey • Almost all your punctuation is correct, and is also used to create effect and provide extra clarity to your ideas	5
7	• Real variety in your sentences – their length, structure, etc – in order to get your meaning across • Good control of your use of verb tenses (past, present and future) and used creatively to convey meaning and clarity • You use a wide range of punctuation both to organise your work and to create different emphases	6

COMPOSITION AND EFFECT

Level	Indicators	Marks
4	• Your key messages or points are generally clear • Tone of the piece fits its purpose • You make some attempt to get the interest of the reader/audience • You use some stylistic features to get your message across, or make writing entertaining or lively • You convey the attitude of the writer/narrator clearly, except where your intention is to make this mysterious	1-3
5	• The material or ideas you select are almost always relevant to the task (even in stories) • You almost always maintain an appropriate tone (e.g. serious tone is not suddenly undercut by comic language, unless you do so deliberately and effectively) • You capture the reader's attention consistently • You use stylistic features to add interest to text (e.g. strong descriptions in narratives)	4-6
6	• You maintain the reader's attention in different ways, not just by good use of language or ideas, but also through changes in mood, use of surprise, etc • You use a range of stylistic devices to create an effect in the reader, e.g. use of direct questions, or keeping information back. • Very clear viewpoint (except where deliberately kept hidden)	7-9
7	• Where you alter the tone of your piece, it is done so deliberately to create a different impact on the reader • Your viewpoint as a writer remains consistent, but other views/attitudes are shown or developed • Reader is engaged and/or entertained throughout • You have an individual style in the way things are described or conveyed, through unusual or original use of language, and clever use of structures • Your writing clearly fulfils the purpose of the task throughout	10

SPELLING

Level	Indicators	Marks
4	• Your spelling of simple and common polysyllabic (many syllable) words is usually accurate • Where you make errors, they are likely to be through using complex homophones (words with similar sounds but different spellings) such as *course/coarse, braking/breaking, threw/through*, etc • You might make errors when you use certain suffixes and prefixes (*tryed, familys, dissapear, hoping/hopeing/hopping, etc*)	1
5	• Your spelling of words with complex, regular patterns is usually accurate (*biography, autograph, geography, etc*) • Where you make errors, they are likely to be through incorrect hyphenation (e.g. *re-act, grand-father*) • Possibly some errors in more complex suffix formations (e.g. *responsable, physicly, basicly*)	2
6	• Most of your spelling, including of irregular words, is usually correct. • You might make some errors with words containing unstressed vowels (e.g. *dependant, definately, discription*) • Some errors possible with consonant doubling in some more complex words (e.g *embarrasement, adress etc*)	3
7	• Virtually all your spelling, including that of complex, irregular words, is correct. Any mistakes stand out as very unusual slip-ups.	5

MACBETH SHORT TASK: EXAMPLE 1

Sentences generally accurate and punctuated properly

Sentences tend to start in same way; little variety

Expanded noun phrase

Spelling

Apostrophe used properly though perhaps a bit chatty/informal

Attempt to engage reader's interest with 'spooky' description

Spelling

You should've been there it was an incredible sight. It all starts when we got off the school coach and we could all look round the old town. Me and James climbed these steps up to this park and it was dead creepy. There were **shadows everywhere and suddenly the sun went in** and you couldn't see anything.

Then James shouted, 'Look!' and we saw this old beggar man with this **old chipped bowl** and he was stirring it round and round. He started saying this chant **aloud** and then suddenly he **dissappeared**! We went up to where he was but there was nothing left. He had vanished into thin air but on the ground there was this old coin which we **dicided** to take to the museum.

Focus	Comment	Mark
Sentence structure, punctuation and text organisation	Most sentences are grammatically correct, and use of paragraphs is simple, but clear. Punctuation is simple (full stops, exclamation and speech marks) but all used accurately. Lack of greater range keeps mark down.	1
Composition and effect	Some attempt to interest the reader by description, and the story itself is well structured making the reader wonder what will happen next. Repeated use of words like 'old' could be improved. Good detail – 'old chipped bowl'	2
Spelling	Mostly accurate, but some common mistakes	1

Overall Level: This student's work falls into the **Level 4** band.

Macbeth short task: Example 2

Variety of sentence starter used

Attempt to engage interest of reader with questions

Prefix error on word; should be 'encircling'

Apostrophe error

Variety of sentence lengths for effect

Good choice of vocabulary to show man's way of speaking

Comma, or other punctuation, missing from this sentence after 'dune'.

Amongst the sand dunes we could see a pool of water. By **it's** side a man was bending down drinking. Sip. Sip. Not desperately, but slowly.

We approached him and asked him where the path was, he looked up at us. There was fear in his eyes.

He began to **garble** a strange language, and then pointed at the top of the sand dune. On the sand dune we saw a man on horseback with a dagger drawn! **Who was he? And why was he following us?** We were just honest tourists who had wandered away from the pyramid.

'Let's get out of here' I said

'Yes, let's' said Aidan.

So, we scrambled down the dusty dune but then we saw the man **incircling** us on horseback. Now he was shouting something. He looked very angry indeed! He was cursing us.

Focus	Comment	Mark
Sentence structure, punctuation and text organisation	Sentences are varied, but occasional lack of control and missing punctuation. Attempt to start sentences in different ways. Some shorter sentences for effect.	3
Composition and effect	Good attempt to engage the reader by giving details of the man by the pool and his way of drinking/look of fear. Vocabulary reasonably varied too ('garble'). Use of questions to make the reader curious, but the end is a little weak.	2
Spelling	Mostly accurate, including more irregular words such as 'honest'. Error on 'it's'.	2

Overall level: This student's work falls into the **Level 5** band.

MACBETH SHORT TASK: EXAMPLE 3

Short opening sentence draws reader in

Abbreviated sentence – no verb – for effect

Single verb for effect

New paragraph for girl

Reader drawn in – wondering what it is

Phrase sums up both child and situation

The journey had been a long one. We had **trecked** along the coastal path for five miles, and hardly seen a soul. Perhaps it was because it was winter, and one of the more isolated parts of the west coast. Around us flakes of snow brushed our red cheeks, and an icy wind gathered pace and began to **sing its grey song. Then**, **a stone in my shoe**.

'I've got to stop,' I called to David, my brother, several metres ahead. He turned, and stood, buffeted by the wind. Behind him, the peak of the hill rose, like **a dark animal, brooding and silent. Waiting**.

It was as I bent down that I saw her. Perhaps it was because I was at ground level. I'll never know. Or perhaps some other, darker force drew my gaze in her direction.

She was sitting on a boulder, low to my right, **cradling something**. I looked up to call **David**, but **David** had disappeared over the peak of the hill. The girl looked directly at me, and I was drawn to her, like a creature pulled into a web.

I stood in front of her, and looked down at the seated figure. She was dressed in a **dark, tattered cloak**, and smears of dirt lined her brow. Her eyes were those of a wild animal, cornered. **Despite this**, she looked directly at me. My own eyes, though, were drawn downwards to the bundle in her arms. Slowly, she pulled the covering back, and the pinched-up face of a baby stared up at me, half-sleeping, half-awake, **caught between two worlds**. I stepped back in shock. For despite the clothing, the strange girl, and the place, there was no doubt about it. **The child was my own son, whom I'd left behind with my wife in our modern London flat a week ago.**

Spelling error – uncommon word - 'trekked'

Vivid image/metaphor

Expanded noun phrase and simile creates ominous feel

Repetition of 'David' a bit clumsy

Expanded noun phrase to give detail

Connective at start of sentence lends variety, and creates link

Surprise ending makes reader want to continue

Focus	Comment	Mark
Sentence structure, punctuation and text organisation	Real variety of sentences: long, short, some with many clauses. Punctuation used both for organisation and effect. One example of unnecessary repetition ('David'). Paragraphs used to telling effect.	5
Composition and effect	Original and varied use of language ('sing its grey song') and strong, vivid details that stay in the mind ('pinched-up face' etc). Draws reader into strange and mysterious situation	9
Spelling	Accurate throughout except for the one error – 'trekking', which can be seen as uncommon.	4

Overall level: This student's work falls into the **Level 7** band.

TWELFTH NIGHT SHORT TASK: EXAMPLE 1

Suffix mistake

Comma should be full-stop or joining word

Reports of this sort tend to be impersonal and don't use 'I'

Error on consonant doubling and homophone

Reasonably clear information in first paragraph

Punctuation here mostly correct, 'though misuse of comma again, and new line needed for speech

Final paragraph used to sum up report, but a little clumsily expressed

WRONGFULL ARREST!

A man called Mr Piper has been wrongly arrested because the police thought he was someone else. Mr Piper is 79 and they thought he had stolen a car, he was driving it up a motorway the wrong way!

I asked Mr Piper what he thought. He said 'It was awful, they should think before they arrest an old man like me' 'But why didn't they realise?' I asked him. 'I don't know. I must look evil or something,' he replied.

Anyway everything was sorted out later when the real Mr Piper was found. He is 17. The older Mr Piper is now **aloud** to go back to his family. The police **appologised** but Mr Piper is still angry.

Focus	Comment	Mark
Sentence structure, punctuation and text organisation	Most sentences are grammatically correct. Clear, if rather basic, use of opening and concluding paragraphs. Punctuation is simple (full stops, exclamation and speech marks) but generally used accurately (apart from commas). Lack of greater range keeps mark down.	1
Composition and effect	Not much attempt to interest the reader by description, but a sense of Mr Piper's feelings comes out through the speech. The basic details of the report are there, although the style of a news report is not quite right.	2
Spelling	Mostly accurate, but some common mistakes (*aloud/allowed, apologised, etc*).	1

Overall level: This student's work falls into the **Level 4** band.

Twelfth Night short task: Example 2

Attempt at suitable headline

First paragraph contains key information; second paragraph builds on it

Common spelling errors

Mistake on 'it's'

Effective rhetorical question to finish

Sentence expanded by use of commas and extra information

Sense of newspaper's outrage through short question to reader

Appropriate use of direct and speech from Mr Piper

PENSIONER PIPER ARRESTED!

Mr Dennis Piper, aged 79, from Grange Road, was imprisoned yesterday by the police after they mixed him up with someone else!

This **incredible** story came to light only after they arrested the real criminal, **who had the same name**, but who was aged 17.

Unbeleivably, OAP Mr Piper was arrested for stealing and driving a police-car the wrong way up the M62 motorway! **Whatever next?** A baby arrested for sucking **it's** thumb?

Mr Piper was very, very annoyed, as you would expect.

'It is awful in this day and age that basic human rights are not respected. How can police mix up the description of a man like me with a teenager?'
How indeed?

Focus	Comment	Mark
Sentence structure, punctuation and text organisation	Variety in length of sentences, and almost all punctuation correct (except for 'it's). Punctuation also used for effect (exclamation marks; question mark at the end)	5
Composition and effect	Range of stylistic devices (e.g. rhetorical questions) and sense of newspaper's outrage will interest readers. Perhaps more information on the story required. Very clear viewpoint from both Mr Piper and paper, but no comment from others involved. Style broadly correct for such a report	8
Spelling	Rather more spelling errors than might be expected at this level, though generally accurate. 'It's' is a mistake of grammar rather than of spelling	2

Overall level: This student's work falls into the bottom/middle of the **Level 6** band.

TWELFTH NIGHT SHORT TASK: EXAMPLE 3

Appropriate headline; use of alliteration

Appropriate 'news' phrase

Direct speech: witness statement interwoven into story

Direct quotes interwoven with indirect speech

Rhetorical devices to make point: strong image, question, etc.

PIPER PAYS THE PRICE

This **morning**, local police are coming to terms with the fact that they falsely imprisoned a **79 year-old man** after mistaking him for a 17-year old joy-rider who shared the same name! **Mr Dennis Piper**, of **Woodland Street**, was arrested after a youth sharing a similar name and address, stole a police car, and drove it the wrong way down the M62 motorway. Police got a name from their computer, without realizing that they were after Lenny Piper, aged 17 of Woodley Avenue, who has a **string of convictions**. The police assumed that Mr Piper, **a senior citizen who doesn't even have a driving licence**, had stolen the car.

'**They bashed down my door, and dragged me away without letting me finish my cup of tea**,' he explained, as he left the police station this morning at 9 o'clock. Local police chief, Chief Inspector Bungle **explained that** just because someone was rather advanced in years, it didn't mean they weren't capable of serious crimes. However, he later admitted that there had been an '**error of judgement**' and that he would be taking '**appropriate action**'. What is clear is that no one will resign over this fiasco, and **yet again**, local police will get away with crimes of their own.

How can it be right that a decent, innocent man ends up spending a night in a **dark, cold cell**, while the real culprit (who is well known to the police for similar offences) walks free on the streets?

It is to be hoped that the police **cough up** some compensation quickly for the older Mr Piper. Who knows, perhaps he can spend some of the money on driving lessons, and find out what all the fuss is about having a car!

Key information in opening sentences: who, what, where, why, etc

First paragraph perhaps too long; could be broken into two.

Extra information placed between commas to expand sentence

Indirect speech used for police comment

Phrase indicates view of writer without his/her name being mentioned

More light-hearted end and look to the future rounds off report, but emphasises paper's view at same time

Focus	Comment	Mark
Sentence structure, punctuation and text organisation	Good variety of sentences in terms of structure, length and how they are started – all used to convey meaning and information. Verb structures used creatively and fluently (i.e. *It is to be hoped...*), fitting the style of such a report. Opening paragraph perhaps a little too long and complicated.	5
Composition and effect	Clear range of stylistic devices (e.g. rhetorical questions) and sense of newspaper's outrage will interest readers. Also, choice of language (*cough up*) is entirely appropriate for a news report.	10
Spelling	Spelling accurate throughout.	4

Overall level: This student's response falls into the **Level 7** band.

HENRY V SHORT TASK: EXAMPLE 1

Spelling

Paragraph clearly answers what Ali has been asked

Some variety in sentence starters

Good cause and effect links

Opening lines are perhaps unnecessary and don't fit with situation

Spelling: letter missed out

Further basic spelling errors

Strong concluding sentence using imperative ('Beware..')

To: Jo
From: Ali

Hi and thanks for the message. **Hope you are well and evrything is fine**.
Here is some **advise** on your question. This is a very difficult situation and it is easy to make a quick **decison**. **But** I think you should think a long time first. **After all** this person may have problems, he may be addicted to some drugs or something or he might be under pressure from a **freind** to do this. I think you should talk to this person quick.
   If after you speak to him or her **then** you find **their** is no real reason for their behavour then go ahead, call the police.
   But **beware** that you may be making an enemy for the future.
   Hope this is good advice. See you soon.

ALI

Focus	Comment	Mark
Sentence structure, punctuation and text organisation	Sentences generally accurate, and some variety in openings. Text organisation is good with a clear sequence of paragraphs. Some sentences a little blunt and not linked with others.	2
Composition and effect	The e-mail does give advice but starts and ends inappropriately. Also, the rather clumsy *Here is some advice…* reads like an essay answer rather than a real piece of advice to an employer.	2
Spelling	Quite a few errors, some of which are of some common, high-frequency words, others which might be homophone/grammar mistakes (e.g. *advice/advise*) Not accurate enough for a mark.	0

Overall level: This student's response falls into the **Level 4** band.

Henry V short task: Example 2

To: Jo
From: Ali

Re: request for advice from me

Dear Jo

Hi! This is **sertainly** a **difficolt** one, and I hope the advice I offer is ok.

I guess their are several options: first, do nothing – and let this guy (I assume it's a guy, or am I wrong?) get away with it. Second you deal with it harshly and get the police **envolved**, and third is a sort of halfway house. You know, threaten him with the police – or make him sign some sort of promise. This might work but I'm not sure 'cos who knows what might happen?

But maybe I need to know more. How did you catch him and what did he say and did he have reasons for doing this awful thing?

Tell you what I'm **gonna** say? Go for it. Hit him hard. After all it was theft. And we saved hard for that new CD player.

There! That's my view.
ALI

Good style to start – not coming on too strong; offering several options (use of colon)

Spelling error

New paragraph changes focus and asks further questions

Rather blunt ending perhaps doesn't suit advice so well?

Spelling errors

Perhaps this sentence needs breaking up or further punctuation?

Again, this sentence seems to contain several points that need punctuation.

Informal use in this context is fine, and the short sentences hit home

Focus	Comment	Mark
Sentence structure, punctuation and text organisation	Sentence grammar is accurate, but several sentences need punctuation to clarify meaning and aid fluency. However, elsewhere punctuation is used helpfully (exclamation marks, colons).	3
Composition and effect	The e-mail gives advice, but the style and overall tone changes a little. It starts in unthreatening advice mode, then switches to a more persuasive, almost angry tone. Not sure this works.	4
Spelling	Although most simple spellings are accurate, there are a number of errors, in common areas such as 'their/there'. The spelling error have the effect of making this response look worse than it actually is.	1

Overall level: This student's response is borderline **Level 5/6**.

HENRY V: EXAMPLE 3

Use of personal pronoun and strong verb sets tone for text

Both sides of situation described in order to create clarity

More informal use of verb makes point

Short linking phrase to link with point in previous sentence

Clear advice given, but use of 'we' involves reader in decision.

Typical 'advice style' phrase fits tone of piece

Single spelling error – consonant doubling

Vivid, idiomatic phrase makes point clear

Colon used to introduce range of possibilities for reader to consider

Use of 'if' and 'then' links action and conditions

Use of modal 'might' expresses possibility, but not certainty: makes advice seem considered

To: Jo
From: Ali

The situation you described to me is clearly very difficult, and **we need to consider** the consequences of any action we take very carefully. **On the one hand**, a crime has been **commited** and the culprit has been caught, and in normal circumstances we would contact the police without a moment's thought. **On the other**, no harm has actually been done, and we have to look at **the wider picture**.

Our club doesn't just cater for the well-behaved, decent teenagers from 'nice' backgrounds. No – we welcome teenagers who perhaps haven't been given a chance to have their own place to talk and socialize. OK, so this person abused our trust, but if we **kick him or her out** and call the police, perhaps we will be setting in motion **a spiral of problems**. You say he or she has promised never to do anything like this again. Is there any way we can find out if they have a track record – have they done this sort of thing before? **If so**, then perhaps we should be less lenient, and call the police in. But I wonder what you would think of the two of us spending some time talking to this person. Perhaps we could find out why he or she wanted to steal**: was it for kicks? Or to buy something? Or were they put up to it by someone else?**

The fact is, we need to know more. If we are going to act, **then** we need all the facts, and I feel that before you pick up the phone and condemn this young person, we should sit back and reflect. We **might act** in haste, but there is a young person's future at stake. I am not saying we should do nothing, but whatever we do do, must be done when we have considered all the angles.

I hope this has been of help,
Ali

Focus	Comment	Mark
Sentence structure, punctuation and text organisation	There is a range of different sentences, some long, some short – all used for effect and to convey advice fluently. Paragraphing is well-organised with each paragraph having a different purpose. Verbs and tenses controlled very well.	6
Composition and effect	The overall tone is just about right; there is a good mix of informal and vivid language, and more formal choice of words and phrases. Realistic details and background also help make the piece sound convincing. An e-mail of this sort might perhaps be a little less formal, and less like a report/business letter.	9
Spelling	Spellings are accurate throughout, apart from the one error on 'commited/committed' which looks like a simple slip.	4

Overall level: This student's response falls into the **Level 7** band.

Section B - Reading

The whole task is **marked out of 18**. Remember, marks are awarded for:

Your **understanding** of the Shakespeare play you have studied.

It is **not** an assessment of writing – although you should remember that your ideas and understanding are shown through your writing, so you should ensure those ideas are **clear** and **well expressed**. Before you look at the mark scheme and model answers you should go back to your answer and see if it is written as clearly as it can be.

Now, use the following tables as a broad guide to the levels you might achieve. Bear in mind that the tables do not cover every skill and idea, so you will have to make a judgement about how close you are to a particular mark or level.

MACBETH: READING TASK

Use this table as a broad indication of the sorts of points and responses you might have made.

Level	Indicators	Marks
4	A few simple facts and opinions about Macbeth and Banquo, possibly saying they were 'sort of friends' to start with but then later on Macbeth starts to 'hate him' and decided to kill him. Some explanation of what is said, supported by some quotations but not always relevant, and rather clumsily inserted into the answer. Perhaps some reference from second extract to the 'fears' about Banquo (*There is none but he/Whose being I fear*) but more reference to the plot than further understanding.	3-5
5	Greater understanding of Macbeth's attitude to Banquo, and how Macbeth invites Banquo in Act 1, Scene 3 to speak together. (e.g. *Macbeth tries to get Banquo on his side for what he has planned*). Some general idea that by the next extract Macbeth has changed – he has killed, and is prepared to do so again. He is now cunning, and already planning his former friend's death (*Macbeth is already planning to kill his old friend because he asks him how he is going to spend the afternoon.*) Some reference, though limited to Macbeth's monologue and what he thinks of Banquo though this might be a little basic (*Macbeth thinks Banquo is a very good person. and is also brave, so he can't trust him anymore...*)	6-10
6	Closer and more detailed examination of the language used in the two extracts, and what occurs and what this tells us about the two men. More reference to their responses to the witches, and how Banquo seems more critical of the 'forces of darkness'. A more secure sense of the changes that take place between the two extracts perhaps with reference to what Banquo has done and said in-between (*Banquo already suspects Macbeth because he has said at the start of Act 3 that Macbeth must have 'played most foully' to be king..*) Focus on individual words and phrases related to the two men (Macbeth's references in his monologue to Banquo's *royalty of nature, wisdom, valour* but also that he envies Banquo's future sons being kings.)	11-12
7	Clear development of the points above with focused analysis of Macbeth's possible attitudes to Banquo, perhaps pointing out that we cannot know for sure that he hadn't already made up his mind about Banquo in Act 1 Scene 3. Clear distinctions drawn between Banquo's greater morality and the effect this has on his relationship to Macbeth, and reference to the Mark Antony/Caesar allusion, if relevant. Quotations wide and varied, and good knowledge of the play as a whole and this relationship's part in it. Perhaps reference to the appropriateness of words such as 'fruitless' and 'barren' to Macbeth, in light of what we come to know of Banquo's children succeeding him, even though he dies.	13+

MODEL RESPONSE
Act 1 Scene 3 Lines 98-155

Act 3 Scene 1, lines 19 to 73

What differences are there in Macbeth's attitude to Banquo in these two extracts?

Strong opening introduction referring to their relationship

Nice phrase to describe change

New point introduced by new paragraph

Point is developed and made relevant to essay question

In Act 1, Scene 3 Macbeth and Banquo appear at first to be **equal partners**. They are **both faced** with the same strange vision on the heath, even though the audience have **already learned in the previous scene** that Macbeth is to be granted the title of Thane of Cawdor. But, we also soon learn that **the seeds of discord** have already been sown between them, as both have been promised different things – Banquo to be **'lesser than Macbeth, and greater..'**, whilst Macbeth is promised immediate power – Thane of Cawdor, and King **'hereafter'**. In addition, Banquo seems more at ease with the Witches, saying he does not 'beg' or 'fear' their 'favours', perhaps already signalling his moral superiority.

Both Banquo and Macbeth are, nevertheless, **taken aback by the news** that Macbeth has been granted the title of Cawdor, as predicted by the witches. **However**, Banquo's response is to mistrust the 'instruments of darkness' **while** Macbeth seems to be already planning his next step with his mysterious statement, 'The greatest is behind'. What is clear is that **Macbeth already suspects** Banquo is a future rival ('Do you not hope your children shall be kings?'), and as his mind explores the possibilities of power, he is beginning to wrestle with how he might acquire it. Nevertheless, he is still unsure whether he needs to act, or wait for power to come to him:

> **'If chance will have me King
> Why, chance may crown me
> Without my stir'**

And most importantly, he has **not yet resolved his feelings about Banquo**. He ends the scene, inviting Banquo to speak privately with him about what they have experienced:

> **'Think upon
> What hath chanced, and at more time,
> The interim having weighed it, let us speak
> Our free hearts each to other..'**

First point developed

Shows knowledge of earlier scene

Variety of quotations to support point

Differences between them drawn out again

Macbeth's 'attitude' to Banquo referred to

Longer quotations supports point about Macbeth's current uncertainty and then his attitude to Banquo

By the time we reach **Act 3, Scene 1**, things have moved on to **the point of no return** between them. In **Act 2 Scene 1**, Macbeth has sounded Banquo out without ever actually saying what he might do, and by the start of Act 3 Scene 1 Banquo clearly suspects his friend of murder and having 'play'd most foully..' for the throne.

In this extract, Macbeth is already planning the murder of Banquo, and is keen to know his movements and plans for the day:

> **Macbeth: Ride you this afternoon?**
> **Banquo: Ay, my good lord.**

Macbeth covers his tracks by appearing to want Banquo at the feast, but the **true nature of his attitude is revealed by the monologue** following Banquo's departure. The equal partner who might have been part of his plans is now to blame for the murder!

'For Banquo's issue have I filed my mind…'
he says.

At the same time, Macbeth **grudgingly appreciates** Banquo's '**royalty of nature**' and the '**dauntless temper of his mind**', almost as if Macbeth wishes he could have been as morally strong. Banquo has 'wisdom' and 'valour', but all these things lead Macbeth not to confide in his former friend, but to fear him, and blame him. This monologue is only broken by the **appearance of the murderers**, and it is apparent quite quickly that Macbeth has been planning Banquo's fate.

In conclusion, we may believe that Macbeth had always known Banquo was a threat to be dealt with, but there is enough evidence from the first scene to suggest that things may have turned out differently had Banquo reacted more positively to Macbeth's advances, or shown a different attitude to the 'forces of darkness'.

TWELFTH NIGHT: READING TASK

Act 2 Scene 3, lines 83 to 143
Act 4 Scene 2, lines 20 to 69

From these two extracts, what different impressions do we get of Malvolio?

Level	Indicators	Marks
4	A few simple facts and opinions about the impression given of Malvolio (*Malvolio is boring and doesn't like people having fun...*)Some explanation of what is said by Malvolio and the others, supported by some quotations but not always relevant, and rather clumsily inserted into the answer.	3-5
5	Greater understanding of how Malvolio makes a different impression on the audience in the two scenes – for example, saying that he is *in charge* and *very full of himself* but that later he is made to look a fool again by Feste and is put into prison. Perhaps too much focus on the different events – Malvolio telling Sir Toby, Maria and the others off in the first scene, then the roles being reversed in the second extract. Some use of quotations, but still not used very well, and perhaps not used to develop new points or ideas.	6-10
6	Closer and more detailed examination of the language and events in the two extracts, and what occurs and what this tells us about Malvolio. More reference to the individual words and phrases used by and about Malvolio (reference to him being an 'affected ass' and a 'puritan') and how our impression of him is created by his actions in the first scene (e.g *Malvolio appears like a stern parent telling little children off..*) and contrasting this with later on (*However, by the second extract he is to be pitied..*) Nevertheless, still seen in quite a simplistic way, and may not refer to the fact that the audience might still dislike and laugh at Malvolio in the second extract.	11-12
7	Clear development of the points above with focused analysis of the relationship between Malvolio and the audience. Quotations will be wide and varied, and good knowledge of the play as a whole will be shown (ie *Olivia's mourning may be seen as a reason why Malvolio acts as he does...*). In addition, perhaps the idea that the impression Malvolio creates is dependent on whether the actor playing him makes him completely ridiculous and unpleasant, or whether he is seen as someone who is trying to do his job in difficult circumstances, and that Sir Toby and Maria are not without blame. Also, contrast between the simple, humble language Malvolio speaks in the cell (*'I think nobly of the soul..'*) with his desire to impress Olivia and others elsewhere.	13+

MODEL RESPONSE

Introduction is clear and focused

We see **two very different Malvolios** in these two extracts. In the first, he believes himself to be the key figure in the household, despite the fact that Olivia has already told him he is '**sick of self-love**'. Nevertheless, she seems incapable so far of existing without him, sending him after Viola/Cesario with the ring, and using him as her 'protection' from the outside world. So, it is no great surprise that in Act 2 Scene 3 he takes it upon himself **to sort out the wild behaviour of Sir Toby and friends,** and when he appears he speaks simply and to the point..

Reference to earlier in play

Explanation of what Malvolio does in this scene

'**My masters, are you mad?.....Is there no respect of place, persons, nor time in you?**'

Quotation to support the point being made

Point is confirmed and then developed, adding an alternative view

It is easy to see Malvolio, **therefore**, as a bit of a **kill-joy**, and this is clearly the response he gets from Sir Toby, Maria and the others. In his defence, **an audience might feel he is justified** – after all, Olivia is supposed to be in mourning, and it could be said that he is merely doing what she asks. However, this doesn't take into account the 'self love' Olivia has mentioned earlier. Sir Toby accuses him of being '**no more than a steward**' – a **glorified servant** – and that he alone cannot make the world '**virtuous**'. In other words, it is arrogant of Malvolio to think the world dances to his tune, and when he threatens Maria by saying he will tell Olivia that Maria allowed this 'uncivil rule', his fate is sealed. He issues a similar threat to Sir Toby. Therefore, the audience no doubt sides with Maria as she catalogues Malvolio's faults: he's a '**puritan**', '**an affectioned ass**', he thinks everyone who '**look on him love him**' and so on. From this moment, this is how we come to view Malvolio.

Further quotations and points support the view of Malvolio in this scene

Strong focus on individual quotations that build view of Malvolio

Switch to how we see Malvolio in the later extract: new paragraph

However, a very different Malvolio emerges in Act 4 Scene 2. From ruling the roost, and believing Olivia loves him, he has been cast into prison and his sanity questioned. The **audience may already feel some sympathy** for the man who believed he was loved, now that he is in this predicament. They may even feel, as Sir Toby appears to, that the joke has gone too far. As he says, **'I would we were well rid of this knavery..'**, even if this is for his own sake, not Malvolio's.

New perspective offered about Malvolio

Quote supports new point made

In this scene, we hear Malvolio pleading with 'Sir Topaz' (Feste disguised) – **'Good Sir Topaz, go to my lady!'**. We also hear him speak plainly and without 'self-love' of the 'soul', when he is questioned. Sir Toby and Feste continue to play tricks upon him, telling him there are transparent **'bay windows'** when, of course, the cell is dark and windowless.

Further quotations and references to what happens build understanding of how we view Malvolio

Ultimately, our impression of Malvolio and our attitude towards him is governed by how much we feel he deserves such treatment. Was his arrogance really so bad that he deserved this? Do Maria, Sir Toby and Feste go too far? Finally, we can say that we see two very different men in these two extracts – but our impressions of them will be dictated by other things, such as **the interpretation of the role by the actor** who plays Malvolio.

Conclusion signalled by 'Ultimately..' sums up the different impressions we have, but also raises new questions, and refers to the role of the actor

HENRY V: READING TASK

Act 3 Scene 1 (not Chorus) Lines 1-34
Act 4 Scene 7, lines 45 to 104
What different impressions of war are given in these two extracts?

Level	Descriptors	Marks
4	This answer will be a basic one which focuses more on obvious things such as the fact that Henry makes a powerful speech (e.g *Henry's speech is good because it makes his soldiers want to win..*) rather than what it suggests about war. There will be some retelling of the story and the fact that the English have won, and some simple descriptions of the battle-field being full of dead people. There may be some use of quotation but it won't always be relevant, and may be used rather clumsily, or without much thought as to specific words or phrases.	3-5
5	An understanding will be shown that the first speech makes war *sound exciting* and is positive and uplifting, with some basic quotations used. Also some awareness of contrast with what Montjoy says, but still quite basic. Perhaps reference to the 'blood' on the battlefield, but little sense of Henry's own change in language, or his confused state – reflecting war itself.	6-10
6	A real sense of the different impressions given of war with clear reference to some of the images used by Henry in his first speech – the 'game', the sport of the occasion, the references to animals (greyhounds, tigers) etc. Quotations mostly used relevantly and skillfully inserted into sentences, all building towards a general point being made (such as how war is presented as noble sport in the first extract, and bloody reality in the second)	11-12
7	Strong insights into the impression of war given in the two extracts and going beyond summary of the ideas and events in order to speculate on why Henry speaks as he does, and also digging deeper into issues such as the way he incites his men to 'lend' their minds and bodies a warlike 'aspect'. Clear sense of contrast with Henry's exhausted and confused state (as it might be played) in the second extract and a sense that war is not straightforward, and rarely noble. Focus on key images such as the wounded horses, the repetition of 'blood' in Montjoy's speech and Henry's own simplicity of language. Also, the way war brings together the noble and the common man, both 'drenched' in the same blood – everybody equal in death, perhaps.	13+

MODEL RESPONSE

Introductory paragraph sums up Henry's intentions

In Act 3 Scene 1, Henry attempts to **stir up the passions** of his soldiers as they launch their assault on Harfleur, and in so doing he presents battle and war as a **glorious, mighty adventure** fought by friends against a common enemy.

This impression is created in many ways, throughout the speech. '**Dear friends**' appears in the first line, mirroring the later mention of the '**band of brothers**'. But war is also seen as something for which you need to disguise yourself – that in a way, it is a type of act…'disguise fair nature with hard-favoured rage..', and he accepts it is not natural to behave like animals (**imitating the 'action of the tiger'**) and that his soldiers need to 'conjure up the blood..'.

Perhaps these are the words of a man who knows that his soldiers would fall back if they really knew what battle and war can do, and that it is easier to put on a mask to fight, and pretend you are someone else doing these terrible things.

However, this is seems at odds with Henry's reference to them being born of fathers who were **used to war** ('war-proof') but nevertheless presents war as a noble cause, that has been **handed down through generations**. The reference to Alexander (the Great) adds to the myth. In addition, it is worth noting that Henry appears to be talking to his nobles – the richer lords and dukes who support him, saying they should be 'copy now to men of grosser blood..', in essence suggesting that war can be used to educate and improve these poorer souls (the 'good yeomen' of the end of the speech) **Finally, Henry compares his men to eager dogs** ('greyhounds') waiting to start the 'game'. The noble adventure is about to start.

Development of main ideas with reference to other sections of play

New points about the type of people the soldiers are

Contrasting point in which Henry calls upon family tradition, and legend

Ends with a final reference to war as a game or sport played by noble people.

Strong opening line immediately tells us student sees sharp contrast in second extract

Key quotes support the point and develop it

Conclusion neatly sums up ideas and repeats the contrast between the reality and the fantasy, especially in the change in Henry's language and what he says

Key point supported by evidence from a different character

Student draws attention to a key specific image to make a point about how awful war is

How different the image of war is in Act 4 Scene 7! Henry's entrance follows the killing of the boys, and he immediately orders that they 'cut the throats' of their prisoners. Not so noble, now. This different perspective of war is emphasised by **Montjoy's graphic description of the battlefield**. There is no mention of a game or sport, just a '**bloody field**', and the nobles '**soaked in mercenary blood**.' Peasants (the 'vulgar') are drenched with princes' blood, too, and there are wounded horses ('steeds') who '**fret fretlock deep in gore..**' (a **horrible image of wounded animals** unable to stand, but kicking out their hooves at dead bodies).

In the end, **war is not clean and tidy** or exciting. Henry, until this point, doesn't even know who has won..'I know not if the day be ours or no..' and on hearing he has triumphed there is no great speech, just a simple 'Praised be God..'

This is the reality of war, not the poetic fantasy.

Overall assessment for the whole paper

When you have assessed your own work, and given yourself marks for each section of the test, you can use the grids below to estimate the level you would gain.

Bear in mind that this is an estimate only and that each year the exact thresholds (differences between levels) change slightly. Therefore if you come out with a Level 6 (especially if you are on the borderline) this does not mean you will definitely get a Level 6 in the final test. However, it is a good indication that you will not get a Level 4!

Overall reading levels

Shakespeare marks	Reading paper marks	Total	Approximate Level
3-5	7-10	10-15	4
6-10	11-15	16-26	5
11-12	16-20	27-32	6
13 +	21+	33+	7

My reading level

Overall writing levels

Shorter writing task /20	Longer writing task /30	Total/50	Approximate Level
2-3	4-9	6-13	4
4-7	10-14	14-22	5
8-11	15-21	23-32	6
12+	22+	33+	7

My writing level

What next?

Question: **Now that I have done the Practice Paper, what should I do next?**

Answer: Doing the Practice Paper should have given you a good indication of where your strengths and weaknesses lie. For example, if you did poorly on the Reading Paper (*Are you being served?*), there's a good chance you need to do a number of things, namely…

Read a wider range of texts – newspaper reports, articles, and other non-fiction, as well as fiction. If you mainly read magazines and non-fiction texts, perhaps you should read more novels and poetry.

Question: **What if I struggled on the Shakespeare reading paper?**

Answer: Did you *really* know the two scenes you have been set?
Have you really got to grips with the *individual words*, and *phrases* used, and most importantly, what they tell us, the reader/audience, about the character who is speaking, or about the issue he or she is speaking about?
How well did you use quotations? In fact, did you use quotations at all? Remember: if you make a point you should try to support it with a quotation or example from the extract.

Question: **And what about the shorter writing task – suppose I struggled with that?**

Answer: The key there is to be quite clear *who* the text is for, *what* its purpose is, and the appropriate *style/language* to go with it. If it's a formal report, does it *sound* like a formal report? If you are asked to give advice, is that what you have done? Or did you just analyse the situation *without* giving advice? Finally, was your writing clear, accurate, spelled correctly and written in coherent paragraphs?

Question: **Is this the same for the longer writing task?**

Answer: Of course, the only difference being that you have more time, and have a planning sheet to help you. Make sure you use it. Those who do their plan and stick to it, usually get higher marks.

Question: **Have I covered everything?**

Answer: Probably not! It's impossible to cover every possible question, every type of text that might come up, but the key is, don't panic. If you prepare wisely, following the advice in this book, and what you have learned from doing the Practice Paper – and, of course, what your teachers tell you, you should do well.

Good luck!